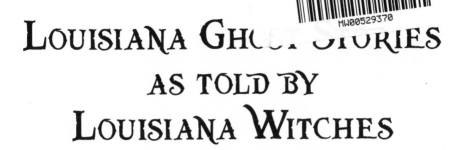

LOUISIANA GHOST STORIES
AS TOLD BY
LOUISIANA WITCHES

EDITED BY LAW

LEFTHANDPRESS
NEW ORLEANS, LOUISIANA USA

ISBN: 978-0615715070

United States • United Kingdom • Europe

CONTENTS

Publisher's Foreword

Witches and those of other faiths share so much.
We are all more similar than different.

Our bodies present a good starting point to examine some of these similarities. Physically we usually have a single head, one trunk, and a variety of dangling appendages. We walk on the ground and look toward the sky, when we trip, we cry and, as aptly illustrated in the stories situated in the Myrtles, we all enjoy a good adventure.

Spiritually all religions share the goal of increasing happiness and decreasing suffering. The Wiccans and all of their great relations including Buddhists, Hebrews, and Christians seek to make the world we all live in a better place. Even the flagellants whipped themselves in this life so that they could enjoy the pleasures of the next life.

Mentally we are united by an abiding curiosity, a fascination for the unexplained and the potent surprises it offers. This collection of stories is largely based upon and illustrates this fascination. Curiosity is a demanding mistress and much is concealed under her oft billowing skirts. The point is not to explain but to abide in mysterie. Explanations are of greatest value when they open vistas of even greater mysterie. The orbs of light which appear in a number of the stories are illuminated as much by an external intelligence as by the observer's own inquisitiveness and interest.

This same fascination with the unknown is also a great driving force behind scientific investigations. Unseen worlds beckon both the scientist and the Witch. Methods may differ but the goal is the same, the illumination of mysterie. The unseen world of the biologist consists of microbes and denizens so tiny and complex that only an electron microscope can chronicle their fantastic travels. The unseen world of the physicist is even more fantastic. These more eccentric offspring of the alchemists with their blackholes and particles moving faster than the speed of light seem to present an interface between the Witch and the materialist. The spirits and other manifestations in these stories are just a bit...just a tiny bit...more illusive than quarks.

We all deserve equal protection of our physical, mental, and spiritual well being under the law of this land. Therefore, there is LAW and there is the publication you now hold in your hands. Left Hand Press will donate its share of the royalties from this publication to LAW for the defense of the comparatively few and, by extension, the defense of us all.

In the past, all of the great religions suffered persecution from lions to burning stakes. These great cruelties of the past and the more hidden but still greatly damaging cruelties of the present now expressed in religious discrimination and prejudice must not be tolerated.

Left Hand Press is proud to in a small way partner with LAW in this Great Work.

Variety in Union,
Union in Diversity.

Dr. Louie Martinié, content editor
Left Hand Press

INTRODUCTION

LAW conceived the idea for this book in 2009. The conception was still a long way off from reality. It began with a Ghost Story Writing Contest in which contestants were offered a prize for the writing of a true ghost story. Some of the best submissions appear herein. After the Ghost Story Writing Contest as word of this project spread, other Witches contributed their submissions as well.

The project ground to a halt for quite some time while LAW sought a publisher. By the grace of the Goddess, serendipity provided the fortunate coincidence that brought LAW and this publisher together. From there, the project took on a life of its own and rushed itself to print as if the stories herein could no longer wait to be told.

All of the stories were written by Louisiana Witches. The paranormal is not a stranger to Witches, and their perspectives on the supernatural are substantially different from their cowan, non-Witch, counterparts.

Generally, you will find in the stories contained herein that, whereas cowans flee from a paranormal experience, Witches embrace it. Similarly, they understand what is happening around them, and, therefore, can offer a better explanation as to what is happening within their stories.

It may be hard to explain the thrill that a Witch finds when he or she encounters a paranormal event. While others flee such situations, many Witches rush boldly forward in an effort to meet the supernatural.

It might be described as that basic fight or flight reflex that people encounter in times of stress. Where cowans tend to exhibit the flight reflex where the paranormal is concerned, Witches tend to exhibit the fight reflex. That reflex is not to suggest that Witches fight the supernatural, but rather that they embrace it. It is not surprising to expect this reaction from Witches because so many Witches walk this world with one foot on this mundane plane of existence and with the other foot on the astral plane of existence.

You can see a little bit of that astral plane of existence in a person's aura. Anyone can learn to see an aura. One common exercise that many Witches learn is how to see auras in people and things. Frequently, they next learn how to control their auras.

With these lessons learned, another common exercise found amongst Witches is one in which one Witch will stand before other Witches while the other Witches tell the Witch standing before them what color her aura is. The Witch who started the exercise then changes the color of her aura without telling the others the new color of her aura. The others then advise the Witch who is changing her aura's color what the new color is. This process is repeated several times. Then a new Witch is selected to stand before the other Witches and change the color of her aura and so on until all the Witches present have had a chance to stand before the others and change the color of their respective auras.

Watching such an exercise is a real eye-opener, especially for those that are just beginning their journey on the path to learn the Craft because such an exercise cannot be faked. There may originally be some doubts by the casual observer, but once that casual observer is trained to see auras and participates in the exercise that casual observer realizes that there own observations and their own aura's color changes cannot be faked. As the saying goes, seeing is believing.

You will find that the stories in this book contain more than just a recitation of peculiar events, and the terror of facing the unknown which terror typifies a cowan's interpretation of the same events.

It should be pointed out that although the stories are true stories, the names of the individuals and the places where the events occurred have been changed to avoid any potential copyright issues.

LAW hopes that you enjoy reading this book as much as it enjoyed editing it.

The Haunted Bed*
by Anonymous

My sister, Angelique, and I lived together when we were much younger and starting to make our way in the world. Like most people at that time of life, financial resources were limited to say the least.

You cannot always be choosy when you are young and broke, and just starting out on your own. Sometimes you just have to take what you can get, and what my sister, Angelique, could get when she needed a bed was her choice of the bed frames that were broken down and stored in Mom's attic.

"Take any one you'd like," Mom said. Angelique picked a simple one, just a plain wooden bed. It was obviously old, but it would not look out of place with the more modern furniture in our new place. She took it home, set it up, and fell thankfully into it at the end of a long and exhausting day. Her sleep, however, was not as restful as she might have wished.

"I had the weirdest dream last night," she remarked over coffee the next morning. "There was this wrinkly old lady, with long, stringy white hair and bony fingers, reaching for me, and I felt like I couldn't get away. Then right before she grabbed me, I woke up."

We did not think much of it, at the time. Everybody has

---

* This story was LAW's 2009 winner of the Ghost Story Telling Contest.

9

nightmares sometimes. This nightmare must simply be a new home, exhaustion nightmare.

About a week later, Angelique was looking a little out of sorts and admitted that she had not been sleeping well. "I've been having that same nightmare, with the old woman," she said. "Every night!"

I told her I thought that sounded like more than a coincidence, and that maybe something else was going on.

"You and your woo-woo stuff," Angelique scoffed. "You know I don't believe in any of that. What's going on is that I shouldn't eat Chinese food before bedtime." But somehow she did not look entirely convinced.

"Maybe I should smudge your room," I offered. "Just in case."

"No," Angelique said. "You keep your religion on your side of the house. I don't want any part of it!"

And that was the end of the argument. But it was not the end of Angelique's nightmares. Over the next few weeks, she dreamed about the end of the world, she dreamed about being shot in the neck, she dreamed about her own death, and she still dreamed about the old woman reaching for her. She would wake up at three in the morning and hear someone breathing in her room or cabinet doors opening and closing by themselves.

Our two cats, Ian and Fatty, who were normally drawn towards any soft and forbidden sleeping place, adamantly refused to go anywhere near Angelique's bed, even when invited. They refused to enter her room, but they would hiss from the doorway at things we could not see.

I do not know what made her start to think the bed itself might be connected to the trouble she was having sleeping in it. She was not admitting her suspicions to me or to anybody else. But she took to sleeping on the couch, and she slept peacefully there.

Her boyfriend had never shared her nightmares on the occasions when he stayed overnight and slept beside her. He thought she was nuts, and he did not hesitate to say so. He also did not hesitate to sprawl across the entire bed and sleep there alone--just once.

About four in the morning Angelique, sleeping on the couch, woke to his voice in her ear, "Baby, move over." He reluctantly admitted to a vivid nightmare of a man in a white mask trying to grab him. He never mocked Angelique's fears again nor did he ever sleep in that bed again.

On another occasion, one of Angelique's high school friends spent the night. She offered to take the couch, but Angelique, of course, insisted she could have the bed. Barely an hour later, Angelique's friend appeared in the living room, asking to make up a pallet on the floor. When pressed, she described a dream identical to Angelique's recurring nightmare of the white-haired old woman, and she slept on the living room floor rather than return to that bed.

Several weeks passed without incident, while nobody slept in the bed. Angelique's skeptical nature and logical mind somehow convinced her that she was being ridiculous and that sleeping on an uncomfortable couch when a comfortable bed lay empty in the next room was irrational. She was a grown woman, after all, and grown women sleep in their own beds in their own rooms.

On the morning when everything came to a climax, I had left for work around 7:30 a.m. Angelique had worked a late shift and was still sleeping when I left. I had been at work for no more than a few minutes when the phone rang. "Stephanie, you...you have to come home right now!" The panic in my sister's voice was all I needed to hear, and my face was all my boss needed to see. I turned around and went straight home.

When I got home, I found a white and shaken Angelique sobbing into my pillow. "Oh my god, what happened?" I asked.

It was a while before Angelique calmed down enough to tell me the details. After her shift at work, she had spent a restless night in her bed, disturbed once again by her recurring nightmare.

Exhausted, she had finally gotten to sleep around daylight.

Just after she heard me leave for work, she felt an uncomfortable weight at the foot of the bed. Thinking that one of the cats, probably Fatty, had finally graced her bed with his presence, she ignored, for the moment, the sense that there was someone else there.

A few minutes later, she rolled over to check the time on her bedside alarm clock. As she returned to her former position, she glanced toward the foot of the bed and realized that, while she could still feel the weight, there was no cat on the bed.

Suddenly, at that same moment, she felt a crushing, oppressive weight pressing her down into the mattress. She was completely awake and alert at this point, but she was unable to move, scream, or even breathe. After what seemed like an eternity, but could only have been minutes, the weight was just as suddenly gone. She had no sense of it gradually lifting or lessening; it was just gone, all at once!

She immediately jumped up, grabbed her phone, ran into my room and closed the door, which is right where I found her when I arrived home.

"Stephanie, I want that thing out of my house! It's evil! We have to get rid of it!" Angelique said adamantly.

Technically, the bed still belonged to our mother, so I suggested we call her and see what she wanted us to do with it. To us it was an unwanted, haunted object, but to her it might still be a family heirloom. It was our grandmother who answered the phone.

"Mawmaw, Angelique has one of those beds from Mom's attic, and she doesn't want to keep it anymore," I said. "Do you think Mom would like it back?"

"Which bed is that, Chere?"

"Just a plain wooden bedstead."

"You have the wooden bed?" she exclaimed.

"Yeah. What about it?"

"Well, if it's the one I think it is, that bed belonged to my mother, and she slept in it pretty much all her life. That's the bed where she used to dream about the Snake Lady."

"Snake Lady? Who's she?"

"Sometimes she was just an old lady with white hair and bony hands; other times she'd be covered with live snakes. Mama would be lying on her side of the bed, the left side, and she'd see the Snake Lady next to her on the right side, or she'd see the snakes crawling all over. When Mama passed, the bed came to me, but I surely didn't want it in my house, and I guess it just got put up in your mom's attic."

Startled by this revelation, we described to my grandmother Angelique's recent experiences in the bed and asked for her advice. Her recommendation was to surround the bed with a ring of salt and burn it.

But when we suggested that we bring the bed out to the country where both her home and my mother's home are located, and do exactly that, she was horrified. She did not want the bed on her property, and she certainly did not want it burned there.

At this point my mother arrived home, so we asked her what she would like us to do with the bed. Her "waste not, want not" ethic would not allow her to destroy a serviceable piece of furniture so she told us to break it down and put the bed back in her attic. At her request, we did just that.

There, as far as I knew, it stayed for a long time. Then, one holiday season, we were up in mother's attic getting down the decorations, and I noticed there were no beds stacked against the wall.

"Mom, what happened to that bed that Angelique used to have. You know, the one that belonged to your grandmother?" I asked, dreading what her response would be.

"Oh, we really needed the room up here, and no one in the family wanted that old thing, so I put it out on the curb. Someone must have had a use for it. It was gone when we got up the next morning."

I do not know if it is common practice across the United States. However, in South Louisiana, leaving something out on the curb is the local notice that the item is unwanted by the owner and is being donated to the first passerby who has a desire to be the new owner.

I guess we will never know what ultimately happened to the bed or what caused Angelique's frightening experiences. Perhaps the bed, during its long association with my great grandmother, the traiteur, somehow absorbed some of the energy that she worked with and remained a link with that mysterious world which was so familiar to her. Or perhaps the Snake Lady was part of the bed's even earlier history and was drawn to my great grandmother's healing gift.

We will never know for sure. But, if you live in South Louisiana, and, if you are in possession of a plain, old wooden bed of unknown origins, perhaps those nightmares of yours are more than just bad dreams after all.

— · —

Author's Note: In French Acadiana a "traiteur" is a traditional healer who uses the laying on of hands and prayer sometimes combined with herbal, magical and faith healing practices drawn from the diverse ethnic groups that have settled this area from colonial time until the present. Most traiteurs view their healing abilities as a gift from Yahweh and incorporate their Catholic faith. Many traiteurs specialize in a particular type of malady or ailment.

My own great grandmother, Ester, treated folks with symptoms related to heat. She could cure sunstroke (coupe-de-soleil), reduce fevers and heal burns. Despite, or perhaps because of, her devout Catholic faith, she had a lifelong, intimate connection to the spirit world. She would routinely ask, "Guess who visited me last night?" as if she were speaking about a family member dropping by, when she was, in fact, talking about a spirit visitor!

Pub Ghost
by Robert MacGowan

There are rare moments in a person's life where one experiences something so RIGHT IN YOUR FACE that you sit there and say to yourself, "Oh My Goddess, they're real." One such moment happened to me in Houston, Texas in 1992. I had just moved to Houston from Phoenix, Arizona after my job transferred me to a satellite office. I promptly found a wonderful, English Pub simply called the Pub.

The bottom floor contained a very nice restaurant where Coats of Arms hung upon the walls along with rich medieval tapestries and a few suits of armor placed here and there. Up a winding staircase was the Pub. British memorabilia was everywhere. The Pub served a fantastic shepherd's pie, fish and chips, and, most importantly, some really great beer.

Over the few following months after I had found the pub, I became friends with the night manager and began staying after hours on the weekends. I frequently remained with the staff until the pub closed somewhere around 2:30 am. At that time of morning, typically, only the manager, an engineer and the bartender, Melissa, remained. Okay, so there were other reasons I liked to stay late, but that's another story which is in no way unnatural.

It was one of these late nighters when I was drinking a German

Pilsner facing Derrick, the manager, when this story begins. Looking past Derrick, the back wall had several booths set up for dining. From the right side of the room, a thick mist drifted past about the speed of a slow walk. My jaw must have hit the floor because Derrick looked over his shoulder and asked, "What's the matter?"

"Oh, nothing," I said, not wanting him to think I was drunk.

Derrick replied, "By the look on your face, you must've seen something. What was it?"

"I just saw a mist float across the room over there," I explained as I pointed to the place where I had seen the mist.

"You're not alone."

"What?"

"Well, you're not the only one to see that sort of thing here," was his matter of fact reply.

Now I was intrigued. "Tell me more," I said.

Derrick then said, "Back in the Fifties, this building used to be a foreign consulate. An envoy and his family lived here with his staff."

"What country's consulate was it?" I asked.

"You know, I don't know," Derrick responded.

"Did anything unusual occur in this consulate?" I inquired.

"Yeah! One day, the envoy's young son fell from the second floor balcony to his death. It happened up there," Derrick said pointing to the spot. "They say his spirit still haunts the place. Several people have reported seeing and hearing weird noises.

"There have also been several accounts from patrons and vendors alike about seeing something strange or the appearance and sudden disappearance of a young boy. In fact, several of my vendors' drivers refuse to return to the bar because of their encounters with a boy who was there one moment and gone the next."

At this time of my life, I was working for a company that had an infrared thermal camera, and I had access to that camera. I got permission from the owner to do an Infrared sweep of the bar and connected buildings.

Now you have to understand, that back in the early Nineties, infrared cameras were not what they are now. They were big, bulky behemoths with grainy images. Who knows, I may have been one of the first ghost hunters to ever use infrared cameras to hunt for ghosts. Though a good effort was put forth, nothing turned up during the investigation, and I put the matter aside for lack of any supporting evidence.

However, just a few weeks later another patron had an encounter, and, Goddess willing, I was fortunate enough to be there. It was nearing closing time, and I was talking to Melissa, the bartender. Suddenly, this bushy, red-haired guy, who looked like the twin of David Crosby of Crosby, Stills and Nash, popped his head into the window next to Melissa.

I had never seen the guy before, but he obviously knew Melissa because he quietly asked her, "Um, Melissa, do you have something OTHERWORLDLY living here?"

Melissa shivered and said, "Oh no, now what?" This question was not the first question Melissa had heard from a bar patron about the ghost, and each time she heard about strange occurrences at the pub, a chill went down her spine. This time was no exception. I could see her shiver as this David Crosby twin said the word "OTHERWORLDLY". Obviously, Melissa was not particularly enamored of the ghost of the son of the envoy.

In response to Melissa's question, the guy said, "Well, I was in the bathroom downstairs, and I was finishing up my business, and coming back up here. Well, I hadn't been through the bathroom more than two seconds when like...I don't know how to explain it... but I ran into...it was like a WALL OF AIR."

"A wall of air?" I said in a rather surprised tone.

He said, "Yeah, it was thick and tangible. I kinda bounced off of it."

"Wow!" I said.

Laughing, he continued his story, "Well, you know, I wanted to be cool, so I said to the Wall of Air, 'Well, here I am. Let's talk.' But man, I was scared shitless. And as soon as I started talking to the Wall of Air, it just disappeared like it had never been there. But then the air around me started getting cold...real cold...you know like freezing cold.

"I was still trying to be cool about the whole thing, so I start to go to the stairs to come back up here. But let me tell you, I hadn't gone more than a step before I lost it. Man, I came up those stairs so fast, like you don't know. I musta took four steps at a time."

We laughed for a bit about how fast he came up the stairs.

Then I said, "You know, when a ghost manifests itself, there's frequently a temperature change associated with the manifestation."

He said, "What?"

"Like what just happened to you. When a ghost appears, the temperature gets cold around the area where the ghost is."

"You think it was a ghost?" he asked.

I could tell he was still shaken by the whole experience. I explained to him what had happened to me and asked if he would go back downstairs.

He replied, "Not without somebody with me."

"I'll go with you," I volunteered.

So, I followed him down into the restaurant. He walked over to the spot where he had encountered the Wall of Air and said, "This is where it was."

He did not have to elaborate. I knew he was referring to the location of the Wall of Air. I could see he was nervous about being back here, so I followed him to where he was standing. I felt nothing. There was no wall, and the air at that location of the restaurant was the same temperature as the temperature upstairs in the bar where we had left Melissa alone.

"Well, whatever was here is gone now," I said stating the obvious. Nevertheless, the David Crosby twin seemed to relax just a bit because of my comment.

    That was my last encounter with the ghost of the pub. As far as I know, the ghost of the envoy's son still haunts the Pub.

Our Haunted House
by Robert MacGowan

My family and I moved from the southwest to Louisiana about ten years ago. At the time, my youngest daughter was seven years old and the oldest twelve. From the very beginning we were experiencing strange happenings.

My wife would hear a young child crying or talking. She had asked our youngest daughter several times if she was crying or talking, but she was not.

We would also see animal shadows. This was not the first time I had seen animal shadows when no animal was present. But that is another story. Particularly, we would see the shadow of a large dog.

One time I felt someone come up behind me when I was at the kitchen sink and turned expecting to see my wife, but there was no one there. I called out to my wife, and she was in the living room watching television.

On several occasions my daughters would have sleepovers, which would end up with one of their friends getting spooked by something they saw or felt.

Here are three examples of things that were so "Here I am" it was almost funny. My wife, youngest daughter and I were going shopping, so we locked our big, chocolate Labrador and our marshmallow of a Jack Russell, Terrier mix in the girl's room to keep them out of trouble. When we got back, the two dogs were outside of the girl's room with the door locked from the inside!

Two weeks or so later the three of us were headed out again when suddenly this loud noise came from the girls' bathroom not ten feet away. My youngest daughter said, "That's my hair dryer," and she went in to shut it off. The selector was on high and the switch was hard to move as most of them are.

The third event was in our bedroom. We were watching a movie on television. While watching the movie, my mustache trimmer in the bathroom turned itself on.

Of course, my first reaction was, "What the hell is that?"

My wife identified the noise first and responded, "Its your shaver."

I got up to see what was going on, and as soon as I got to the door of the bathroom, the mustache trimmer turned itself off.

I turned to go back and watch the movie, and it came on again. At this point, I said something like, "Okay, now you have my attention," and then I went into the bathroom again. As soon as I turned the light on, the electric shaver turned off. There it was, still in its charging stand looking as innocent as could be. I was not buying it.

Since then, the touch lamp on my side of the bed will be off one moment and on the next. Usually just on low. There have been a few times where my wife would find it on high.

We live in a house that was only ten years old when we moved in and from what we could tell nothing unusual or traumatic had happened there, so this leads me to believe that these strange events are connected to the land.

Cat Shadows
by Robert MacGowan

As the Witches biggest Sabbat, Samhain, (more commonly known by cowans as Halloween) rolls around, it sometimes brings out warped and sadistic people who think that torturing and killing animals is fun. Of course, only a cowan would think it was fun to torture and kill an animal. A Witch never would.

The particular Samhain I write about was one of the worse when it comes to cowans torturing and killing animals. About fifteen years ago I was living with another Witch, who was both my friend and roommate. I had just finished work and was sitting down at my laptop to finish the days reports when I began to see fleeting shapes out of the corner of my eye. As the minutes passed, the shapes went from fleeting shapes to full-blown, CAT shadows running all over the apartment. I turned to my roommate and asked, "Are you seeing this?"

She replied, in frustration, "I don't see anything."

She suggested that I should call downstairs to the apartment below where a few others of our kind were and ask them if they were experiencing anything unusual. So I did just that.

One of my friends answered the phone, and I asked for the High Priestess who was down there at the time. I was told she was busy, and then she asked, "What's up?"

I responded, "I'm seeing shadows of cats fleeting across the walls of my apartment." I was told to hold on, and the High Priestess was quickly put on the phone.

It turns out that they were working magick to help guide the spirits of the animals that had been killed to cross over. I was told to tell the spirits that I was seeing that we were there to help and everything was okay.

I did so, and, as quickly as the cat shadows had appeared, they were gone.

Strawberry Plantation
by Shadowspawn

I have been a Witch for over twenty-five years, and very few supernatural occurrences bother me. However, every once in a while, a paranormal experience is unsettling. I recount one of those herein.

Some years ago, a friend of my wife's invited us to house-sit with her and a mutual friend. The four of us met at the house.

My wife and I had come with the specific intent to hunt for ghosts because the quite modern house we were house-sitting for was in the middle of what used to be an old, strawberry plantation. Upon arriving, we drove down a long driveway to a beautiful, two-story home that was set way back on the property and was quite secluded from the road.

We met my wife's friend at the front door, and she gave us a tour of the house. The front door led to the living room, which was the main room downstairs. The ceiling must have been at least forty feet high. A couch and love seat were the main furniture in the room. Both pieces focused on the big screen TV.

Right off the living room was the staircase that led to the bedrooms upstairs. We left our suitcase in one of those rooms that had a canopied bed. Then we went back downstairs to finish the tour.

The living room opened to a large kitchen and dinette. In the center of the kitchen was an island with a marble counter top, and it sported a faucet of shining chrome.

The dinette led outside to a patio and a built-in swimming pool and hot tub combination. The backyard was otherwise filled only with a meticulously cut lawn that typifies suburbia and yuppie-dom.

In fact, the most notable feature about the entire place was its spotlessness. I suspect a number of minimum wage employees had replaced the slaves of old. Who had it better off was hard to guess.

The one inconsistency in this otherwise monument to yuppie-dom was the slave shack in the front of the house, which shack was set off to the left of the property. Its wood had rotted over the years as it stood next to an encroaching, bamboo grove.

My wife and I could not resist exploring it. As we approached, we encountered the bamboo grove first. I could not help but feel a strong sensation of malevolence as we neared the bamboo grove. The malevolent sensation was the same when we examined the barren, slave shack. All sense of who had it worse off, the former slaves or the more recent minimum wage employees, left altogether.

The slave shack was boarded up so that we could not enter it, which was just as well because I no longer had any desire to examine it any closer. We returned to the patio as I tried to shake off the sense of evil that I had felt.

It was about dusk now, and we broke out refreshments. We heated up the hot tub, and everyone joined in the frivolity. The night wore on, and, as our skin began to wrinkle, one by one we left the hot tub to relax on the patio.

My wife began taking pictures with her digital camera. The atmosphere was ostensibly frivolous. Nevertheless, the sense of malevolence I had felt earlier began to grow in an intangible way. None of us were even contemplating ghost hunting as the late night turned into the early morning.

Who noticed it first, I do not remember, but, across the backyard where no structures were, three lights shone at the level of a second story window. They were not halogens, neons, or even tungsten lights. By the color of their lights, they looked to be lanterns. Not Coleman lanterns, mind you, but kerosene lanterns.

We considered the lights for some time, but no one suggested leaving the patio to investigate. After a while, the lights not seeming to be ready to depart, we retired from the patio to inside where we watched a movie.

Even inside I sensed the malevolence that had pervaded the evening. My wife seemed oblivious to it, but I convinced her to leave at first light.

It was not until we got home that we reviewed the pictures that my wife had taken around the pool. One of the pictures manifested a skull shaped mist. We have kept the picture and shown it to any who would look at it. Just looking at the picture gives one a creepy feeling.

I have not returned to that house since that night years ago. My wife rarely talks to her old friend as their lives have drifted apart. I believe the owners of that old, strawberry plantation had another home in the city. And I wonder if the spotlessness of that country home had more to do with nobody wanting to stay there than to the cleaning crew.

The First Witch
by Shadowspawn

I was eight years old when I met the first Witch, or more accurately Witch's apprentice, I ever knew. It happened like this.

My father had just retired from the military, and we moved back to New Orleans, Louisiana. I was in second grade, and it was the middle of the school year. My parents rented a house in a posh neighborhood. It was not until the summer that I met her.

A little girl, Francesca, perhaps a year younger than myself, came to visit her grandmother for the summer. My sister and I quickly became friends with Francesca. Shortly after we met her, I saw the first ghost I have ever seen.

I was playing in my backyard in the middle of the day, when all of a sudden and without any warning, I saw a young man, who was transparent, run across my neighbor's backyard and leap into my neighbor's house. Not through a door mind you, but through the side of the house. I never saw the ghost again although I did go to the house it jumped into once.

As one can imagine, the whole sighting was quite disconcerting to an eight year old boy. Obviously, I could not resist talking about it. I told my sister, and she, in turn, told me that Francesca had come to stay with her grandmother for the summer, and her grandmother was a Witch. My sister also said that Francesca's grandmother was teaching Francesca Witchcraft. So my sister and I repeated the whole story about the ghost I had seen to Francesca.

Francesca did not seem surprised at all. She seemed to believe that this sighting was an indication that my sister and I were meant to become Witches like she was.

So at dusk of the same evening, Francesca performed an outdoor ritual, which I will not describe here, initiating both my sister and myself as Witches. Over the remaining months of that summer, Francesca taught us the basics of spell workings if not the entirety. As kids will, I have to admit that my sister and I misused our new found knowledge, mostly to curse each other and defend ourselves from each other's curses, sibling rivalry being what it was between us.

Francesca left at the end of the summer, and we moved to another house in New Orleans the following year. So we did not see Francesca the following summer nor did we see her in the next decade. Though we had not seen her in such a long time, I did not forget Francesca or the lessons she taught us.

But I did see Francesca once more in my life. I was about twenty when a chance encounter brought us together. She was a pentecostal at that time. She had no recollection as to who I was nor did she admit to any knowledge of Witchcraft, which, considering the circumstances, was not surprising.

It was some years later before I did a Dedication Ritual. So I find myself in the unusual position of, arguably, being an Initiated Witch long before I was a Dedicated Witch.

I might rule out that childhood Initiation as being of no import except for two things. First, that ritual initiation at dusk meant more to me than any religious ceremony foisted upon me by my parents' religious choice for their children.

Second, as I learned later or you might say relearned later, Francesca actually had taught my sister and I the mechanics of performing a spell working. And as I said before, my sister and I practiced that new found knowledge for many years with a vengeance that fueled our sibling rivalry. I remember still using those techniques until I was about fifteen.

It was not until I was nineteen that I met the second Witch I ever knew and that my training in magickal disciplines continued and that story too is as coincidental and strange as this one. In retrospect I can see the Lady calling to me from a young age. But that I had the wit to see her then! Still, while I may not have known the whys and wherefores, she was always at my side leading me to her.

The Second Witch
by Shadowspawn

Jonathan was a musician who I first met when I was eighteen. I was a budding lyricist. It did not take long before we started writing songs with great aspirations to make it in the music industry. During the week, I would write lyrics. On Friday night, I would bring them to Jonathan, and, if he had set my prior week's lyrics to music, we would record the song.

As happens from time to time, either Jonathan or I would develop writer's block. On those nights we would just hang out, mostly discussing our latest girl problems. It was not very long until Jonathan introduced me to the Tarot as a way of divining the nature of whatever girl problem I had at the time.

After I was comfortable reading Tarot cards, Jonathan introduced me to Astrology. He gave me a book on Astrology, which, by the way, I still use today, and I was casting natal charts in no time. I purchased a book or two on my own to supplement my fledgling library and started casting more complicated charts like synastries to check for potential compatibility with whomever I was dating at the time. What can I say, I was a healthy red-blooded American male, i.e., my life revolved around women, and I did not hesitate to use my new found divination techniques to help me with the dating process.

Jonathan would review my charts and survey my readings encouraging me when I was doing them right and pointing out my missteps when I was not. Because we were both only nineteen at the time, I should have been curious as to where he acquired his knowledge, but it never occurred to me to ask.

Once when I came over, Jonathan put away some books in a hurry, one had a big, blue cover, but I would not discover what the book was for many years. We delved into much more dangerous magicks, but I was oblivious to danger then and eagerly absorbed all I could. And still, it never once occurred to me to ask Jonathan how he had come by his knowledge.

On one night when I had come over to Jonathan's, he gave me a small object which I was to wear around my neck. He told me to carry it around with me to solve some problem I was having at the time. It had a small chain on it so that it was clearly intended to be worn around the neck. When I objected to wearing it around my neck because it looked strange and because I did not want to have to explain why I was wearing it, Jonathan said it would be quite alright to simply carry it with me.

It was small enough to carry in my pocket. And that is where it ended up.

I have long since forgotten what the problem was, but I have not forgotten the object. After the problem was resolved, I stuffed it in my dresser draw. To this day I still have the same dresser. If I had ever thrown that dresser out, I probably would not have made the discovery that I did.

Like most friends of our youth, Jonathan and I went our separate ways after a couple years of songwriting. I heard he went off to Nashville and then returned to New Orleans, but I never saw him again since those songwriting days.

A few years later, however, I found my way to Wicca. One of the first books I ever purchased on the subject was Buckland's Complete Book of Witchcraft by Dr. Raymond Buckland, Father of Wicca in the United States. The book is affectionately referred to as "Big Blue" due to its blue cover and its rather large size, and it was and is one of the first books many Wiccans or Wiccans-to-be ever read. I read the book from cover to cover and worked the course religiously (if you will excuse the double entendre).

It was not until I completed the coursework that I rushed to my dresser draw and pulled out the small object Jonathan had given me so many years before. It was then that I realized that the small object given to me by Jonathan was made in the manner Dr. Buckland described in his book. It was then I recalled the big, blue book Jonathan had hastily hidden away one night so many years ago. And it was then I realized that I had studied under the second Witch I had ever met.

The Haunted Shack
by Shadowspawn

The Coven I was in at the time decided to spend some time sharpening our ghost hunting skills. The High Priest of the Coven lived on an old plantation. In fact, the Covenstead was on this same property. The High Priest was experiencing some otherworldly phenomenon where the old, slave shacks used to be. Where a row of old, slave shacks used to stand on the property, only one shack remained.

One Sunday morning the entire Coven went out to view the remaining old, slave shack on the property to see if we could sense anything. It was a tiny thing, barely an eight by eight foot square footprint.

Over time, the old, slave shacks had ceased there original function and served as hay storage buildings. So upon opening the door of the remaining shack we found it had several old, mildewed bundles of hay.

Despite the smell, we each entered the old shack. The shack stands about three feet off the ground on piers. So to enter the shack, you have to step up.

Upon entering, I examined my surroundings. It had four walls. The floor was wooden. Six bails of hay lay on the floor in the back half of the shack. There were three rafters supporting the roof. And the only way out was through the door I entered the shack through.

I began to use the appropriate techniques for walking in both worlds, but I felt nothing otherworldly. All the other Witches in the Coven had left the shack, and I, being the last Witch remaining therein, was about to leave figuring there was nothing there to sense. As I turned to leave, an image of a window in the back wall flashed through my mind. It was not an ordinary window, but rather a small door the size of a small window cut into the back wall. It was a window that clearly was not there, but the vision I had just seen was so strong and persistent that I could not ignore it.

I turned around and lifted my hand to the spot on the wall where my vision said a window should be, and I pushed. Much to my surprise, the wall where my hand was spun away on a hinge. Not the entire wall, mind you, but essentially a door the size of a small window rotated outward on a hinge in a deosil direction exactly as the image in my mind had suggested.

The other Witches of the Coven were already outside and were watching me as I pushed open this window. I could hear them gasp behind me as surprised as I was. When I turned around, I asked who had gasped. Though they all admitted to being surprised to see the window, no one admitted to gasping vocally.

The otherworld floodgates seemed to open at that moment. Other Witches in the Coven began to sense things. One saw a female slave being tortured. Another saw a young man torturing another.

We began searching the sides and back of the shack trying to get a further sense of what had happened there. We could only guess that the shack had not been torn down like the other shacks had because some evil persisted there that no workman dared to defy.

Our exploration expanded, and we began walking the grounds further and further from the shack. The High Priestess with us encountered the remnants of what she took to be an old cattle pen. She sensed something malevolent there and called me over to check it out with her.

When I arrived, she explained what she felt, but I sensed nothing other than perhaps a sense of timelessness or a primordial feeling that this area maintained from an ancient time before humans existed.

The High Priestess was obviously uncomfortable, but I was ready to explore further. Against the cautions she was giving me, I prepared to climb over the barbed wire fence at the back of the pen that led off into the surrounding marsh. As I grabbed the barb wire, another flash entered my mind. The flash was a picture of an unspeakable mutilation occurring should I attempt to climb the barb wire fence.

Because my last flash a short time ago was so accurate and because the High Priestess kept begging me not to go into the marsh, I, uncharacteristically, changed my course of action and yielded to the High Priestess' advice and feelings. We returned to the others who were milling around the shack.

Having found what we came for, we left the shack that morning and returned to our covenstead to discuss the morning's findings. We did not finish discussing those events in a day or a week. But when we did finish discussing that Sunday morning's events, we decided to exorcise the malevolent young man's spirit from that slave shack.

We charted our time for the exorcising ritual to correspond with Astological influences. I made an Athame of Gemini so that we could better communicate with the targeted, malevolent spirit. While I have no intentions of discussing the ritual in detail, a few details are noteworthy and described below.

Every one of the female Witches who entered the shack during the ritual turned a ghostly pale and felt as though the malevolent spirit hated and had tortured women. Suffice it to say that those Witches did not remain in the shack for any length of time.

Also, the spirit manifested itself sufficiently when told to by a male Witch to blow out a candle on command.

Perhaps, most significantly, as I examined the shack that night, I had another vision. The vision I had was that of a woman being hanged from one of the rafters.

Finally, magick was worked that night to exorcise the malevolent spirit. I cannot say what happened to the spirit, but I do not believe we were successful in our endeavor.

Quite some time after the events I have just described, the High Priest of the Coven bought some goats to manage the grass on his property. The goats were allowed to roam free on the fenced area of the property which area includes the spot where the old slave shack still remains to this very day.

The High Priest of the Coven told me recently that one of his goats died. It happened this way.

As I mentioned earlier, the old slave shack sits on piers about three feet above the ground. Somehow, one of the goats managed to get underneath the shack, and, still more oddly, from underneath the shack, the goat managed to push her head up through one of the floorboards. It was in this condition that the High Priest of the Coven found her strangled the next morning.

I recalled my vision of a woman being hung from one of the rafters, and he said he had remembered it too when he found the goat that morning. We both concluded that the malevolent spirit was still there. It is obvious to us both that more work remains to be done if we ever expect to remove that malevolent spirit. To this day, it is both unwise and unsafe to visit that old slave shack.

I will also say that I have been on the High Priest's property before and since many times, and it is easy to see that the property has a lot of supernatural entities on it of all sorts. The property is surrounded by swamp. Just walking the perimeter of the property gives one a sense of walking back through time to a primordial period, and a sense that the swamp contains deep, dark secrets that it does not want to share.

The land itself seems to whisper at you that it is angry with humans for the rape of the Earth. Our ghost hunting adventure only uncovered one story, but hinted at many more.

The Myrtles
by Shadowspawn

My wife and I heard that the Myrtles, an old plantation in Louisiana, was one of the most haunted places in America being featured in national television programs. We decided to go ghost hunting there.

My wife booked a room on the first floor of the main house. Booking a room at the Myrtles is an adventure in and of itself. The plantation is always booked well in advance. So it was several months after booking our room that we actually went.

We grabbed all the ghost hunting equipment we had, which included a camcorder, a few cameras, both digital and conventional, a few analog tape recorders, and a laptop computer. In addition to our ghost hunting equipment, we brought enough incidentals to supply a small army for a month.

I have to admit that, though it is usually my wife who over packs, I was to blame in part. I wanted to make sure that we did not miss any ghosts that might appear just because I forgot to bring enough supplies. So I packed extension cords, a large supply of every battery known to man, and enough spare tapes to record the entire series of Dark Shadows.

We arrived about three o'clock in the afternoon. The driveway of the Myrtles features a metal statue of a thin, frail woman. The statue was only about four feet tall. We would later discover that the statue was a life size reproduction of the plantation's mistress.

We found a parking spot and proceeded to check in where we purchased tickets for the tour given later that evening by the plantation staff. After checking in, we began the process of dragging all our gear into our room. Unloading our car looked something like the scene out of Blair Witch II, Book of Shadows, where the crazy tour guide unloads an endless supply of camera cases making the van he is unloading look more like the T.A.R.D.I.S. than a tour bus. An hour later, we were done.

After getting all the gear into the room, we explored the place. Our room consisted of a three room suite. We had a proper southern sitting room, connected to the bedroom which had a walk-in closet. The bedroom was connected to a bathroom. The rooms had electricity, electric lights and modern plumbing, but otherwise it seemed the suite had been kept in its original condition. However, I am not sure whether the interior bathroom was new or part of the original home.

In any event, after surveying the rooms, we decided that the most likely place to find ghosts would be in the bedroom. Rightly or wrongly, the bedroom is where we chose to set up the camcorder. We aimed it at the bed in such a way as to cover the bed and the door leading to the sitting room in the hopes that anything that appeared in the sitting room had a chance of being caught by the camcorder. Throughout the evening and night, I changed the tape in the camcorder every two hours.

By the time we were set up, it was five o'clock and we were getting hungry, so we headed over to the restaurant where we had made reservations. The meal was pricey, but excellent. And the service was unsurpassed. They even let us change tables without question after a mother, whose unruly kids make a case for the re-institution of mandatory corporal punishment for all children, had the gall to take those unruly children out in public and, more unforgiveably, to sit next to us. Much to my disappointment, the restaurant at the Myrtles had closed on our subsequent trip there.

After supper, we toured the grounds. The Ante-Bellum home

was two stories tall and had a porch surrounding it on all sides. Behind the house was a courtyard. The old stables had been converted into suites. The restaurant was in the old barn if I remember correctly.

One of the most striking features of the Myrtles is a man-made lake in which is found a small island connected to the mainland by a wooden bridge. The small island sports a gazebo and a small statute of a cherub.

And of course, the plantation takes it name from the numerous Crepe Myrtles scattered around the property. These trees had been pruned at an early age such that each tree had only one main trunk. The beauty of these trees was not lost, even on me.

After our tour of the grounds and many photographs later, we took the tour provided by the plantation staff. There we saw the bottom floor of the main house, which floor consisted of a foyer, the mistress' bedroom, the men's parlor, the women's parlor and a dining area. The upstairs rooms were rented to guests, so that we did not get to tour them, at least we did not tour them with the plantation staff.

We retired to the courtyard enjoying the ambiance when a stranger approached us. He was middle aged, overweight, but not obese, loud mouthed, drunk and, quite frankly, a bit obnoxious. But I was uncharacteristically polite, and I did not even mention any of my mental impressions to the annoying stranger.

After exchanging names and making small talk in which he made to sure to determine that we had rented a room in the main house, he confidentially told us that he had arranged to visit two of the upstairs rooms after the plantation staff had left for the night. He invited us to join him later for that tour. Of course, we accepted the invitation, after which the stranger did not seem quite so boorish.

We sat on the back porch partying with the stranger and others who had rented rooms in the main house. We all waited for the plantation staff to leave for the night.

When the plantation staff left somewhere around ten o'clock, we toured the two upstairs rooms as promised. What we did not know was that the stranger had found all the people who had rented rooms in the main house and arranged tours of the other two upstairs rooms as well.

After touring those two remaining rooms, we could not in good conscience fail to offer a tour of our suite as well, which we did. We then retired to the back porch and partied with our new found friends for an hour or three longer until one by one we all made our way back to our respective rooms and retired for the night.

We awoke late in the morning, and we sauntered slowly over to a continental breakfast in the courtyard. We seemed to have been the last guests to have awaken that morning. We said our goodbyes to our new found friends and made our way home.

As soon as we got home, we began the arduous task of unloading. An hour later, we were done. However, not even the task of unloading could quell my excitement of finding out whether we had captured any paranormal activity on our tapes and recordings. So, quite naturally, as soon as I had unfinished packing, I began to review the tapes. Prominent in all the tapes were many orbs of various sizes floating helter skelter throughout the suite.

Normally, I am not convinced that there is paranormal activity just because orbs show up on tapes or in pictures. But because we had spent the night in the suite and had seen no insects, one cause of orbs on tapes and pictures, one natural cause of orbs was seemingly reasonably eliminated.

Another natural cause of orbs in tapes and pictures is dust. I imagine there could have been quite a lot of dust in an old plantation, but two things suggested that the orbs were not made by dust.

The first is that the suite we were in was regularly rented and occupied by guests of the plantation. Therefore, it can be presumed that it is regularly cleaned. A regularly cleaned room has a lot less dust than an uncleaned room thereby lowering the chances that the orbs were caused by dust.

The second is in the movement of the orbs. Many of the orbs we caught on tape moved fast and also changed directions more than once. While this type of movement is consistent with insect movement, which movement I had already ruled out, it is not consistent with the movement of dust.

The tapes exhibited one more strange anomaly. The first five minutes of each tape was normal. But after five minutes in, the tapes went blank.

I ruled out the power supply for two reasons. First, the camcorder was running off of AC power and not batteries at the time the recordings were made.

Second, I had changed the tapes several times that night and into the wee hours of the morning. And at no time, did I find that the camcorder functioned improperly or that it lacked power. In fact, I had set an alarm, and I got up every two hours and changed the tape. And each tape, no matter what time it had been inserted into the camcorder, had images for the first five minutes and only the first five minutes.

The camcorder has an auto-focus and that seemed to be the most obvious culprit. But I am not convinced that the auto-focus is the culprit here. First, I could not reproduce the problem at home.

Second, and perhaps more importantly, the lighting changed through the course of the night and morning without affecting the results. When the camcorder was first set up, it was afternoon and the sun was still shining and letting light into the room despite the very thin curtains on the windows. The same is true of the following morning. Of course, as the evening wore on, the sun set, and the darkness was complete.

Finally, the camcorder has a light that automatically shines when the room lighting is too low. So at least at night, there should have been sufficient light to film from the camcorder's automated self-illumination. In fact, when I initially set the camcorder up I tested it to make sure that the automated lighting function worked properly, and it did.

For all these reasons, we should have gotten more than five minutes of filming on each of our camcorder's tapes. That we did not is quite simply unnatural.

While I cannot say with any certainty that we experienced paranormal activity at the Myrtles, I also cannot say that we did not. Both the orbs and the camcorder's strange anomaly remain unexplained to this day.

Samhain at the Myrtles
by Shadowspawn

After my wife and I stayed at the Myrtles, we came back to our Coven and told them about what we found and how much fun we had. The Coven decided to go to the Myrtles when the veil between the worlds is the thinnest, on Samhain or, as the cowans call it, Halloween. This time there would be more focus on ghost hunting.

We had learned from our first experience, and amongst the Coveners was more equipment. This time we were equipped with camcorders, digital cameras, digital and analog tape recorders, an infrared camera and a laptop.

The Myrtles fills up quick. But for Halloween, it fills up even quicker. In fact, the plantation opens its booking one day a year for Halloween, and an hour after the booking opens, all rooms are rented.

Unfortunately, we did not get rooms in the main house, but we did get adjacent rooms in the Carriage House, which used to be the plantation's stables. We met there about three o'clock in the afternoon.

This time we were prepared with both ghost hunting equipment and magickal tools. Again it took about an hour to unload and settle in. After we settled in, we went and explored the grounds.

The placed was packed with people. On Halloween, the Myrtles has more tours than normal, and the tours draw a quite

49

sizeable crowd being a must see ghoulish stop on the Halloween tour circuit.

The restaurant was closed, but, because of the size of the crowd, the plantation had cashed in on its popularity and offered hot dogs, hamburgers and other refreshments. We took our supper in the courtyard.

Dusk comes fast at that time of year and that day was no exception. We took the tour offered by the plantation. And many of the Witches in our Coven sensed presences about us. I personally felt the presence of the plantation's mistress during the tour.

After the tour, we geared up with our equipment and went ghost hunting. We began by placing a protective circle around the grounds. Then it was off to explore.

We walked the entire grounds. We caught nothing to speak of on the infrared camera, but plenty of orbs showed up on the digital cameras and the camcorders. In some of our pictures, the clear night sky was filled with more orbs than distant stars.

Our pictures also revealed mists sitting in the chairs on the front porch of the slave shack. These mists could not be seen with the naked eye. Furthermore, the mists remained in the chairs regardless of the angles from which we took the pictures. We even caught on our digital cameras mists in a couple of the trees, again, mists which could not be seen with the naked eye.

But the most convincing evidence of a haunting was found on the island. Our High Priest, my wife and I had just crossed the wooden bridge to the small island in the middle of a shallow lake on the plantation's premises, when our High Priest pointed back the way we had come to the middle of the wooden bridge saying, "Something is back there on the bridge. Take a picture."

My wife turned and, using her digital camera, she took a picture. Because the picture was on a digital camera, we could review it immediately. Sure enough, a mist could be seen in the picture in the middle of the bridge where our High Priest had pointed, but it could not be seen with the naked eye.

Our High Priest wanted to rule out any possibility that the mist was just a camera anomaly on the picture, so he called out to the spirit, "I see you on the bridge. Come on over here where we are."

Upon his instruction, my wife, who had not moved a step from the position she was in when she had taken the first picture, began to take several more pictures in succession.

By the time she had taken the third picture, our efforts were ruined by a guest of the plantation, not affiliated with our Coven, who came barreling across the bridge yelling, "Jamie! Has anyone seen Jamie?"

However, before that guest so rudely interrupted our investigation, we got two good pictures on the digital camera. The first picture showed that the mist had moved closer to the foot of the bridge when our High Priest had called to it. The third picture revealed that the mist had just stepped off the bridge. This evidence was enough to verify our personal experiences and verified that the Myrtles has an intelligent haunting.

After we had thoroughly explored the grounds, we retired to our rooms. We moved the furniture around to provide sufficient room to perform the traditional Wiccan celebration on this most Holy Sabbat.

After the ritual while still in Circle, we did some experiments in summoning the spirits of the plantation. There were three attempted possessions, but we were well prepared. The summonings were further personal experiences that confirmed our objective findings.

We discussed the evening events for a bit, and then retired to our respective rooms for the night. After a late start in the morning, we loaded our cars with all the equipment and other items we had brought. We checked out barely in time to avoid being charged for an extra day.

On the way home, we all stopped for breakfast at a quaint, local diner. We had cut checkout so close that we had missed our continental breakfasts.

After breakfast, we continued our journey home. After unloading our equipment, we collapsed exhausted, but satisfied that our investigation of the Myrtles had once again been rewarding.

The Curse and the Gift
by Kasey Morgan

My mother always told me that there were women in our family who had a "Gift" and that I was one of them. Being a child this meant nothing to me. I just wondered, "What's a gift?"

However, I did know enough to recognize that I was different from my peers. Although I would join them in their play at times, I was mostly a lone wolf cub cuddled and nurtured by Mother Earth. It was in the forest where there was solace and protection from things I felt but could not understand at the time. Actually, I do not know that I fully understand them now, but I do know things have changed. And one small child went from the cold darkness to the warm light, and she understands that the Gift is a blessing and is always with her.

But though my mother's family is blessed with the Gift, my father's line is afflicted with the "Curse". For a long time, the Curse seemed a lot stronger than the Gift.

For as long as I can remember, even as a small child, I have had dreams. They were always different, but the theme remained the same; a large man in a dark, cape-like garment was chasing me. Trees whirled by as I ran fast as I could. Then, there it was again, the familiar wagon with huge wheels drawn by a run-down whitish horse on a rutted mud road. I do not remember a driver ever on the wagon. The wagon was the kind that poor people might have used in the seventeenth or eighteenth century.

The dark man was relentless, and the ending always the same. He would chase me down, and, unmercifully, he would murder me. Sometimes, he would brutally stab me multiple times. Sometimes, I would be strangled. Sometimes, I would be shot.

My dreams are always sort of grayish in nature. They are colorless except that in each of those dreams, in which I was murdered, the fatal wound always revealed bright red blood flowing like a sticky river down my body. I could always see the color of blood ooze out along with my life. I could feel my heartbeat fade to a flat line.

These dreams plagued me for three decades. My family or, later, my husband would wake me as I screamed and fought in my sleep. The presence was always there surrounding me even after I awoke. The spirit was still in my house. I could feel him as my heart raced and my breath ran rapid as if I had been sprinting. Terrified!

These nightmares always left me so afraid that I would lay awake, so the shadow man did not come back. I never saw his face in all those years, and he never came to me while I was awake.

Then, a strange thing happened eight years ago. The dream came to me as it frequently did, and it was as it always was except for two very crucial details. First, I saw the dark man's face. And second, although terribly wounded, I did not die.

Since then, a new more powerful dream comes to me. Now the dark man is after someone else, and I am the one chasing him down, armed and with a strong fearless heart to prevent his dark intentions.

Violent deaths have been such a normal, accepted part of one side of my family. I have heard it called the generational curse. Others have said we have a suicide gene. So many have died at their own hands. Then there is the moldy shroud over those that struggle with the curse and end their lives "accidentally".

Sometimes I wonder if the dark man successfully visits them

until they can take it no more. The family does not talk of such cursed things, but we all know that we all know this unspoken secret. For myself, I have come to believe that the blessing of the Gift is stronger than the affliction of the Curse. I know that, but for the Gift, like others in my father's family before me, I would have gone.

Somewhere between the dark and light I did encounter spirits that were neither good nor evil. They just were. For instance, my husband and I had booked a night at the Myrtles Plantation which is reportedly the most haunted plantation in America. I had stayed there before and nothing remarkable occurred. This time, however, although I expected nothing, two particular events transpired. They are really nothing impressive; they are just instances of an earthly spirit (me) and non-earthly spirits sharing a particular space at the same time.

The first event occurred so fast and unexpectedly that it left me feeling disoriented. A tour group was entering the first floor foyer and, being last in line, I shut the door and moved on to catch up with the others. After a few steps, in between a huge mirror and a staircase, I felt a "whoosh" go through my entire being from right to left. I stood there shaking my head trying to orient myself when my husband turned back to get me, looked at me funny, and asked if I was alright. I was. It was not a harmful experience. It just was a momentary sharing of a spot on this Earth with an otherworld entity.

Nothing else occurred that evening worthy of mention, but the next day something did happen. I did not even realize what until later. As we were getting ready to leave, I went back upstairs to the bedroom foyer and was videotaping the area. No one was there. There was no sound to speak of except the creaking floor as I stepped about. No big deal.

When we got home, things were different. As we watched the video, noises could be heard of pots and pans being rattled as if the staff was cooking a meal. There was no kitchen in the house.

In fact, kitchens were generally built apart from the main house to reduce the possibility of fires burning down an entire mansion.

Why the tape picked up these noises, where none were at the time the recording was made, is beyond me? I have heard this type of recordings being referred in ghost hunting parlance as EVPs, Electronic Voice Phenomenon.

Lastly, there's the other side of my family, the side with the Gift. In the past eight years, I have come to realize that I am like my grandmothers and have inherited their gift of knowing, seeing and feeling things that others do not. I no longer fight this. I am even proud that one of my grandmothers was a respected midwife in a time when it was not so okay to be one. I have opened myself to the Gift, and spirits come to me from time to time, but they no longer come from a place of evil. I have seen glorious orbs in the forest. I have felt and savored the whispering spirits of my grandmothers as they enfold me lovingly with their being. I am surrounded in goodness now, and it is joyous!

Walking the Grounds
by Cliff Eakin

I have been a third degree Wiccan Priest for so long, I can hardly remember when I started practicing Witchcraft. For quite some time, I owned and managed an occult store in New Orleans, Louisiana.

Hurricane Katrina destroyed the business, and I purchased land in Springfield, Louisiana where I built and run a pagan campground known as the Gryphon's Nest Campground. My church, Coven of the Gryphon Wiccan Church, has often leased the campground to hold church functions that were similar in nature to pagan festivals.

In the course of my practice as a third degree Witch, I have seen many supernatural events. At the request of my good friend and fellow Witch, Shadowspawn, I recount one of those events for you below.

Some time back a few friends of mine purchased some real estate with a checkered past. They asked me to walk the property to see what I sensed there.

"Ai yah yah yah yee," I said as I came to a certain point on the property. "Crazy woman." And I continued to walk on.

A bit further, I came to a well. I looked down it and said, "This was poisoned."

I walked on. As I walked, I came to another area. "Someone's running." A little bit further down the way, I said, "She's a black woman. She's running."

I walked a bit further sensing this young, black woman running. "She's being chased," I said.

As I walked on, a name came to me. "Marlborough," I said, and I continued to walk the property.

Then I stopped. Something felt wrong. I no longer felt the young, black woman running. I walked back the way I had come a few paces. I sensed her again. "The young, black woman died here," I announced to my friends.

I walked further and came upon the remains of a burned down house. In my mind, I saw an image of the young, black woman standing in front of the house holding a baby, her baby. I could tell the baby was interracial. Thus, the reason for her death became clear to me.

I described the woman and the baby to my friends. Though I continued to walk the property, I felt nothing more. We eventually returned to our starting point.

My friends knew the history of the property and wanted to see what I would sense as I walked the grounds. Having done so, they were now anxious to tell me that history.

My friends took me to a small graveyard on the property which graveyard they had not shown me on our previous tour. Many of the headstones contained the name "Tarlborough".

Apparently, the Tarlborough family had owned the property prior to the Civil War. The husband and wife who lived there were unable to conceive. So it came to pass that Mr. Tarlborough ordered a young, black slave of his to bear his child in secrecy.

At the first, the woman refused and ran away. But later, as the story goes, she remembered what her mother had always told her, "Always obey your master," and she returned home. Whether her mother had actually said this or whether the young woman simply got hungry with no place to run, I suppose we shall never know. But in any event, she returned home, and she bore the child as was required of her.

When the child was born, Mr. Tarlborough tried to pass the child off as his and his wife's own child. Unfortunately for him, it was apparent that the child was of African/American descent. And thus, it was equally apparent who the child's mother was which meant that Mr. Tarlborough had lain with a black woman.

In those unenlightened days, such a tryst was the most heinous of sins. The family sought out the young, black mother with murder in their eyes. Seeing them coming, she ran away. Across the property, she ran, but she could not outrun the pursuing family members.

When they caught her, they killed her immediately. The story does not say how, but there can be no doubt what happened.

Mr. Tarlborough's mother, who lived on the property as well, went crazy after the murder, and she poisoned the well that I had earlier located on the property and burned the house where the young, black mother had lived, the burned house I had seen on the property. Everyone in the family died, including the crazy mother, as a result of the poisoned water drawn from the well. The headstones we were looking at seemed to confirm at least this much of the story.

I noticed that the grave of the young, black mother was conspicuously not in the graveyard amongst the other graves. I asked my friends, "Do you know where the grave of the mother is?" My friends knew without further explanation of whom I was speaking.

They replied that they did not know. "Shall we look for it?" I queried. They too were curious to discover where the young slave had been buried, and we agreed to search the property for the missing grave, if any such thing could be found on the property.

Eventually, my sixth sense led us to a remote area of the property where we found a small mound much like those in the Tarlborough family graveyard. And even though there was no headstone to mark it, I was certain this mound was the grave we were looking for.

We stared at the grave in silence for a while, each of us lost in our own thoughts. For my part, I was enraged at the senselessness of my ancestors' ridiculous taboos and the ignominy that had brought this young, black woman to this place because, you see, I am a white man, and my significant other is a young, black woman.

Mischievous Gnomes
by Cliff Eakin

As I have mentioned earlier, after Hurricane Katrina destroyed my occult store in New Orleans, Louisiana, I purchased land in Springfield, Louisiana where I built and run a pagan campground known as the Gryphon's Nest Campground. My church, Coven of the Gryphon Wiccan Church, has often leased the campground to hold church functions that were similar in nature to pagan festivals.

The property also had a house on it where I live. Soon after my Lady and I moved into the house, we experienced strange phenomenon.

It first manifested itself in small ways. Immediately upon moving in, my dogs constantly followed unseen visitors. The dogs looked up to the rafters and barked at strangers we could not see.

Small items moved from the place they were set without explanation. These occurrences escalated into flying objects.

We had a christmas tree mounted in the living room at Yule. The christmas tree is actually a pagan tradition borrowed by the christian church. On at least one occasion, the ornaments flew off the tree across the room.

On another occasion, an entire coffee pot flew across the room at my Lady.

I happened to mention the incident with the coffee pot to my neighbor. She then told me the tale of the previous owner.

It seems the property was up for sale when I purchased it, not because the owner was afraid to live through another hurricane like Katrina. There were many former Louisianans who fled the State for good after that hurricane.

However, in this case, the previous owner was selling the property because of a less natural phenomenon than hurricanes. Apparently, the former owner of the property had had similar experiences to those I had recently had.

Then one day, when the former owner was not home nor anyone else in her family and the house was locked up, something happened. When she arrived home and entered the house, she found all items that had been on the kitchen shelves on the kitchen floor in disarray as if they had been thrown there.

Whether my neighbor's story was accurate or not, I cannot say. However, I accepted the story as true because it conformed to the facts of my experiences.

After hearing this story, I decided that things were out of control and that it was time to take some action. My studies in the Craft suggested a number of possibilities for the source of these anomalies, but my Witch's instinct told me what the cause was, Gnomes!

Gnomes are Earth elementals that can be mischievous if not treated with the proper respect. And I wanted them to move out of my house. Now, trying to force Gnomes to leave your home when they do not want to do so is nigh near impossible. So I did the next best thing.

I went out to my workshop, and I built them a beautiful castle of their own. I placed it on my property in a suitable location near the treeline and close to the swamp.

Then I gathered my coven together, and we performed a ritual donating to the King of the Gnomes the Gnome home, the beautiful Gnome castle I had built. We gave them other presents as well and struck our bargain with Gnomes.

I could tell the bargain had been accepted because during the ceremony I saw a wisp of mist appear beyond the treeline in the swamp as the deal was struck. Since that ceremony, I have had no further incidents of moving items in my home.

And apparently, the Gnomes are enjoying their castle because they refuse to allow it to be damaged. A few years later, Hurricane Gustav swept through Louisiana and caused much property damage. I did not escape that hurricane unscathed, however, the Gnomes did.

After Hurricane Gustav blew through, I surveyed my property. When I came to the Gnome castle, I found it untouched by the hurricane. That condition was rather surprising because I trees had been blown over during the storm on either side of the Gnome castle. Somehow the Gnome castle had not been crushed or otherwise harmed. I am convinced that the Gnome King commanded the storm to pass his own by.

Walking in Old Houses
by Louis Martinié

I have had my dog for a long time. Ever since I was a young girl. I remember a little bit...such a little bit. It was so long ago that I sat with my mother's dog in a room of our house on Dumain Street in New Orleans, Louisiana and something happened.

All that I remember is the shadows; shadows that moved on the pink wall, deep black shadows on the light pink paint. I may have seen more but the shadows are all that I remember. Perhaps it was nothing but shadows.

A man with black, coarse hair came to where we were sitting. He took my mother's dog, and he stood behind it. He dropped his trousers. I was frightened. He had two tails. One in back that was long and had a curl to it. One in front much shorter. I do not know. I was so young, and all I saw was shadows. The shadow that was him looked over at me, and I was frightened. He said, "Now, Mon Chere, there will be a baby. It will grow and protect you."

I was so young. The next thing I remember is a new dog in the house, an awful looking new dog. Its coarse black fur stood out in points. Such an odd dog, but, odder still, only I could see him, and I saw this dog more as shadow than as substance.

My parents were not concerned. Children see such things, and these things go away with age. Their timeless wisdom they shared, and I was comforted by their words, but the dog never did go away. He became familiar to me, and, in a manner, I grew to love him.

He stayed in the front of the house under a chair in the doorway. Such a long time he was under that chair. He protected the house, and he protected me.

People would enter. If he did not like them, he would follow them, a great shadow behind them on the ceiling. A shadow that only I could see. I grew up, and I grew old in that house. I never married, and the house, in time, became mine. Still the dog lay under the chair continually protecting our house.

The rhythm of my life was gentle; I did not rise to great heights. I fell into no chasms of despair. Day followed day, and night followed night in easy procession. I grew old with that shadow dog.

My hair took on the gray color of summer mornings cut through with storms, but the dog did not age. His shadow remained black and bristling on the light pink walls. The pink is from a paint that takes its color from pig's blood, and I know that he draws strength from that pink, though I do not know how.

I remember getting very sick. My old body grew so heavy. Darkness covered me, and then light blinded me. I was confused, and when I woke up I was sitting in the chair in the hallway with the dog beneath me.

Things are different now. People cannot see me or the dog. Still, I sit and offer my un-returned greetings. What else is one to do?

The dog is the same as ever. He follows those who enter my house with ill will in their hearts; a shadow ever behind them. But now I see what he does.

At times it looks to me like he bites their shadows. Ah! They feel nothing. They leave wholly unconcerned, as if all were well, but I know better. Then the terrible bite reveals itself to them, perhaps as a coincidental accident, perhaps as an unexpected illness.

I still sit in my beautiful old lace with the dog beneath me, and I greet those who come to my house. "Bonjour," I say to those who pass my way. Though now, after seeing the aftermath of the dog's bite, often times I add, "Be careful walking in old houses."

(This may be a vision, an old memory or a bit of both. I know not. I do know that one would best show respect when entering the abodes of the dead. L.M.)

Made in the USA
Middletown, DE
18 May 2020